Jan. 2013

Sanitation Workers Help Us

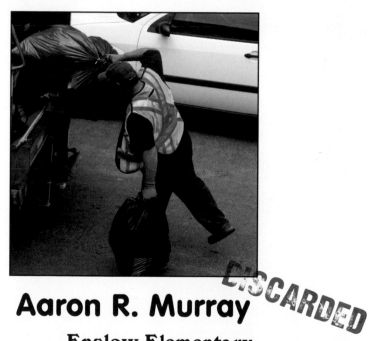

Aaron R. Murray

Enslow Elementary

an imprint of

Enslow Publishers, Inc.
40 Industrial Road
Box 398
Berkeley Heights, NJ 07922
USA

http://www.enslow.com

Enslow Elementary, an imprint of Enslow Publishers, Inc.
Enslow Elementary® is a registered trademark of Enslow Publishers, Inc.

Library of Congress Cataloging-in-Publication Data
Murray, Aaron R.
  Sanitation workers help us / Aaron Murray.
    p. cm. — (All about community helpers)
  Includes index.
  Summary: "Introduces pre-readers to simple concepts about the sanitation workers using short sentences and
repetition of words"—Provided by publisher.
  ISBN 978-0-7660-4049-6
  1. Sanitation workers—Juvenile literature. 2. Refuse collectors—Juvenile literature. 3. Refuse collection—Juvenile
literature. I. Title.
  HD8039.S257M87 2014
  331.7'6136372—dc23
                                    2011037462

Future editions:
Paperback ISBN 978-1-4644-0058-2
ePUB ISBN 978-1-4645-0965-0
PDF ISBN 978-1-4646-0965-7

Printed in the United States of America
032012 Lake Book Manufacturing, Inc., Melrose Park, IL
10 9 8 7 6 5 4 3 2 1

To Our Readers: We have done our best to make sure all Internet Addresses in this book were active and appropriate when we went to press. However, the author and the publisher have no control over and assume no liability for the material available on those Internet sites or on other Web sites they may link to. Any comments or suggestions can be sent by e-mail to comments@enslow.com or to the address on the back cover.

Enslow Publishers, Inc., is committed to printing our books on recycled paper. The paper in every book contains 10% to 30% post-consumer waste (PCW). The cover board on the outside of each book contains 100% PCW. Our goal is to do our part to help young people and the environment too!

Photo Credits: Comstock/Photos.com, p. 22; iStockphoto.com: © EdStock, p. 20, © JeanValley, p. 3 (recycle), © manley099, pp. 3 (dump), 16–17, © Mike Clarke, pp. 1, 6, 12, © Sava Miokovic, p. 18, © Sherwin McGehee, p. 10, © stockstudioX, p. 4; Shutterstock.com, pp. 3 (garbage), 8, 14.

Cover Photo: © stockstudioX/iStockphoto.com

Note to Parents and Teachers

Help pre-readers get a jumpstart on reading. These lively stories introduce simple concepts with repetition of words and short simple sentences. Photos and illustrations fill the pages with color and effectively enhance the text. Free Educator Guides are available for this series at www.enslow.com. Search for the *All About Community Helpers* series name.

Contents

Words to Know

garbage

recycle

dump

Sanitation workers take away garbage.

They help keep our streets and homes clean.

Some sanitation workers clean city streets.

Some sanitation workers pick up garbage on your street.

Sanitation workers
pick up garbage
in snow, rain, ice,
or wind.

Sanitation workers are strong.

They lift a lot of heavy garbage.

DANGER

Garbage can
be dangerous.

Sanitation workers
wear gloves to keep
their hands safe.

They wear bright
clothes, too. This helps
drivers see them.

Sanitation workers take garbage to the dump.

Some garbage
is recycled.

It is used to make
new things.

Plastic bottles
are recycled.

Metal and paper
are recycled, too.

Do you like to
help take out
the garbage?

You are helping
sanitation workers
keep the neighborhood
clean and safe.

Read More

Piehl, Janet. *Sanitation Workers*. Minneapolis, Minn.: Lerner Classroom, 2006.

Trumbauer, Lisa. *We Need Garbage Collectors*. Mankato, Minn.: Pebble Books, 2003.

Zamosky, Lisa. *Sanitation Workers: Then and Now*. Huntington Beach, Cal.: Teacher Created Materials, 2008.

Web Sites

NIEHS Kids' Page: Reduce, Reuse, and Recycle
<http://kids.niehs.nih.gov/recycle.htm>

City of Los Angeles Bureau of Sanitation. *Kids Love LA & Keep It Clean.* <http://www.lacitysan.org/kids>

Index

Guided Reading Level: C
Guided Reading Leveling System is based on the guidelines recommended by Fountas and Pinnell.

Word Count: 121